The Supremacy of Jesus

The Supremacy of Jesus

Lance Lambert

LANCE LAMBERT MINISTRIES
Richmond, VA

Copyright © 2018
Lance Lambert Ministries
Richmond, VA
USA

ISBN 978-1-68389-094-2
www.lancelambert.org

Contents

Preface

The two messages contained in this booklet were given by Lance Lambert in January 2003 and January 2004, respectively, at the International Prayer Conference in Jerusalem. They have been transcribed and printed by permission with minimal editing for clarity. The printed messages have not been reviewed by the speaker. Unless otherwise indicated, all Scripture quotations are from the American Standard Version of the Bible (1901).

1.
The Centrality of the Lord Jesus

John 1:1–5, 14–18

In the beginning was the Word, and the Word was with God, and the Word was God. The same was in the beginning with God. All things were made through him; and without him was not anything made that hath been made. In him was life; and the life was the light of men. And the light shineth in the darkness; and the darkness overcame it not.

And the Word became flesh, and dwelt among us (and we beheld his glory, glory as of the only begotten from the Father), full of grace and truth. John beareth witness of him, and crieth, saying, This was he of whom I said, He that cometh after me is become before me: for he was before me. For of his fulness we all received, and grace for grace. For the law was given through Moses; grace and truth came through Jesus Christ. No man hath seen God at any time; the only begotten Son, who is in the bosom of the Father, he hath declared him.

Colossians 1:12–18

Giving thanks unto the Father, who made us meet to be partakers of the inheritance of the saints in light; who delivered us out of the power of darkness, and translated us into the kingdom of the Son of his love; in whom we have our redemption, the forgiveness of our sins: who is the image of the invisible God, the firstborn of all creation; for in him were all things created, in the heavens and upon the earth, things visible and things invisible, whether thrones or dominions or principalities or powers; all things have been created through him, and unto him; and he is before all things, and in him all things [hold together]. And he is the head of the body, the church: who is the beginning, the firstborn from the dead; that in all things he might have the pre-eminence.

Shall we pray:

Lord, we just want to stand by faith into that anointing which is ours in our Lord Jesus, and which the Holy Spirit makes a living reality. Fill this time, Lord, with that anointing both in the speaking of Your word, the translating of it, and in the hearing of it. We ask it in the name of our Messiah, the Lord Jesus. Amen.

The theme of this conference is "Digging Again the Wells," taken from Genesis 26. It speaks of Isaac digging again the wells that his father had dug and the Philistines had filled up with sand

and debris. It seems to me that in digging again the wells there are some matters of supreme importance to believers.

I think we are in the prelude of some very great fulfillment of God's purpose. The powers of darkness, the principalities, the world rulers of this darkness are in foment. They know that something very big is going to be fulfilled.

Therefore, it is all the more important that we dig again the wells that our forefathers dug. I am thinking now of what has happened in the history of the work of God from Pentecost onwards. And I am not talking about 1903 or 1906 depending upon whether you are British or American. I am talking about *the* Pentecost, Shavuot, some two thousand or so years ago, when God set in motion something in Jerusalem among us who are Jewish and took it by the Spirit of God to the ends of the earth. It seems to me that certain wells were dug, and those wells have been filled up with rubble and sand over time by the enemies of God and the enemies of the purpose of God. It has always been so.

Wherever you look in the history of the true church, the body of the Messiah, there has been a redigging of the wells, whether it was the Reformation, or the Anabaptists, or later the Puritans and Covenanters, or the Moravians, or the Quakers so much later, or the early Methodists. None of these people ever called themselves the names that everybody knows them by today. They were just believers who in some marvelous way redug the wells from the beginning and let the pure water of God flow out again.

Therefore, it seems to me, that if God is going to do something tremendous, that *something* is being contested by the powers of darkness and evil, and will be contested even more in the days that lie ahead. No matter where you turn, the crisis is enormous, but this is the greatest opportunity for the Spirit of God. Therefore, it is very important that we understand why the Lord led us to this theme "Digging Again the Wells."

I want to confine myself to one well that is in danger of being filled with rubble and debris. It is the supremacy and centrality of the Lord Jesus. That to me is a tremendous well. There is not a single movement in the history of the true church of God that has not begun with a new understanding and a new recognition of Jesus as Lord. When He has been enthroned, as it were, a mighty inner spring of living waters has flowed out that has changed nations and the course of history. And it has always begun with a new understanding of the Lord Jesus.

When Mary, saints, or anyone else took the place of the Lord Jesus, the person of the Lord Jesus was demoted, devalued. This was never intended by those in the institutional church, but it came about in some way. Always, when the Spirit of God moved in a new way in the history of the church, it was in direct relationship to Jesus as King, Jesus as Lord, Jesus as Head, Jesus as the source of all, and Jesus as the end of all.

Every departure from the pure beginnings of the work of the Spirit of God in the history of the church has started with a dethronement of the Lord Jesus. That is how important this matter is. Whether it is the church, the individual, or the Christian worker, in the end all is related to the Lord Jesus. I cannot think of any well more important.

There is another well that we must dig again and that is the word of God, for it is precisely the same. When the word of God is devalued, when the word of God is made to be insignificant, when the word of God just becomes dry and dusty ancient literature, nothing happens. But whenever the word of God is recognized for what it is, then it becomes what it is—alive and active. Men and women are born through the word of God. They are changed and brought into a living relationship with God. And once again nations are changed and the course of history is changed.

The Triune God

I am going to give myself to this matter about the Lord Jesus. I want to talk about the problem of the Trinity. This is an enormous problem. The word "trinity" does not even appear in the word of God. Of course, it does not mean that there is not a triune God, but the word "trinity" does not appear. And there has always been controversy over this matter. There are those who read the Scriptures and see Jesus as man. They see Him as a unique man, a special man, but only a man. They see Him as a human Messiah. There are others who read the Scriptures and only see Him as divine. But wherever you turn in the word of God, if you go too far one way, you are confused, and if you go too far the other way, you are confused. The early church defined it in a creed, but we are dealing with something that is essential mystery and can only be revealed to the believer by the Spirit of God.

I only know that as a Jew I have met God in the Lord Jesus. I have discovered in the Lord Jesus, God. I have come into the salvation of God by the Lord Jesus, and every single new experience of God has been in and through the Lord Jesus.

In the early days of the Pentecostals, they only talked about Jesus. It was Jesus, Jesus, Jesus; everything was Jesus. Now it is the Spirit, the Spirit, the Spirit. In the early days of the Charismatics, people fell in love with the Lord Jesus. They knew that they were alive to the Lord Jesus. They heard the Lord Jesus; they obeyed the Lord Jesus. Now it seems more and more that only the Holy Spirit is spoken about.

To a certain extent, parts of the institutional church have made it seem as if there is a pantheon of Gods—three Gods, absolutely separate. This is confusing, especially since the Lord Jesus, when asked which was the greatest commandment of all, answered, "Hear O Israel, the Lord thy God, the Lord is one." It is hard for us to understand. I do not like the word "trinity"; I always speak of the triune God.

Then there are others who have said that Jesus is not merely man but He is less than God. We have a whole wing in the Messianic movement that sort of goes along this line, that somehow or other Jesus is less than God but He is more than man. Personally, I find this difficult, because if the Lord Jesus is some created archangel, how in the world can I be found in an angel and an angel in me? That is very odd. It seems to me some form of spiritism.

I want to open up this whole thing because I believe this is a well that has an awful lot of rubbish in it. There is an idea that we have three Gods. That to me is rubbish. Yet we have one God and three persons. We cannot fully and completely understand this, but at least we have some understanding.

Our Lord Jesus as Expressed in John's Gospel

To help us better understand, we will go to John's gospel. John's gospel is not a synoptic gospel. Matthew, Mark, and Luke, are synoptic gospels. They are histories, eyewitnesses, (or in Luke's case, collated from eyewitnesses), of the story of the Lord Jesus. John's gospel is entirely different. It was not written as a synoptic gospel or as a history, although wherever it touches historical things it is absolutely accurate. John's gospel is an interpretation. It is built in quite a different way. You have a prologue and you have an epilogue. Then you have the whole main thesis of the book built on eight claims or declarations of the Lord Jesus, beginning with I AM, and eight signs. John does not call them miracles; he calls them signs because they are not *just* miracles. They are miracles that signify something of tremendous importance.

The Prologue

In the very beginning of this incredible gospel, which reveals something of our Lord Jesus, we have these words: "In the beginning was the Word, and the Word was with God, and the Word was God." It is an inescapable conclusion that the Spirit of God led John to use these words which parallel the very first words of the old covenant: "In the beginning God created the heavens and the earth." Then he goes on to speak of the Spirit of God brooding upon the face of the waters.

"In the beginning was the Word and the Word was with God and the Word was God. The same was in the beginning with God.

All things were made through Him and without Him was not anything made that has been made. In Him was life."

"In Him was life." I suggest that cannot be an angel. Here you have the supreme attribute of God. In Him was life and the life became the light of men. That is something tremendous. How do you explain it? If Jesus is more than man and less than God, how can you say, "In Him is life"? Only in God is there life. God is the source of all life. I encourage myself every day with that.

I think of Arafat. His life comes from God and in the moment God speaks the word, it will end. It is the same with Saddam Hussein, and the same with you and me. There is a time to be born and there is a time to die. And God is the supreme source of all life. It is almost blasphemy to speak of someone created as being the source of life. In Him was life and the life is the light of men. Is this the word of God? That is why I would like to talk about the word of God as well because some people say, "Oh, be careful of Paul. He was the founder of Christianity, not Jesus. And he was a woman hater. Be very careful of him." I hear it all the time, this kind of nonsense.

Then people will say, "Don't trust John; John is the one who speaks badly about the Jews." Well, I sometimes speak badly about the British. Very often I say to Brits, "So hypocritical." It does not mean that I think that the Brits are absolutely all demonized and no good, but very often you speak this way about people you belong to. So did John.

The Word Became Flesh

"The Word became flesh and dwelt among us." That is mystery. The beginning of Jesus was not in Bethlehem; He had a prehistory. When the Word became flesh and dwelt among us, that was Bethlehem. It began with Bethlehem, but He had a whole eternity before then. It is amazing.

Listen to this. "No man hath seen God at any time" (verse 18). Let it sink into you. "No man hath seen God at any time; the only begotten Son, who is in the bosom of the Father, he hath declared [manifested] [revealed] [defined] him." That is tremendous. No man has seen God at any time. So when Jacob saw the Lord and lived, it had to be the Lord Jesus. And when dear Abraham and Sarah made a meal for three visitors, one of those three was the Lord. You remember how He spoke to them.

No man has seen God. How can any human being see God? Little bit of human debris that I am—finite, small, a flea compared with life in proper—how can I ever see God? God does not have hands or feet. How can I see God? How can I understand God? How can I know God? Here is the mystery of the person of the Lord Jesus. "No man hath seen God at any time; the only begotten Son, who is in the bosom of the Father, he hath declared him [defined him]."

When I first came to the Lord in a sovereign act of God, it was actually through reading the first Christian book I had ever read in my life, *C. T. Studd* by Norman Grubb. That incredible story of a human being who believed that God was to be obeyed changed my whole life.

Nobody ever thought to ask me if I had a Bible. I had no Bible. I had never seen one. I had never read it. I had never been in a place of worship such as a synagogue, chapel, or church. On one occasion, my sister and I did steal into one in Petersham, near Richmond, called St. Peters, and it was full of skulls and crossbones. We both decided that Christianity was all to do with bones, skeletons, and dead bodies, as it were. They were all carved, in stone of course, around the altar and everywhere else. On another occasion just to make sure what Christianity was about, we stole into another place, where an old white-haired gentleman, wearing black, stood in the pulpit speaking to about sixteen or seventeen other old people with white hair. So we decided that Christianity was something to do with death and old age.

The Signs

The first Bible that was ever given to me was a little gospel of John. I read that gospel of John through and through and through until it fell to pieces. One of the things that gripped me, even as a thirteen-year-old boy, was the I AMs. Now I do not want to be irreverent, so I want to be very careful, but Jesus was either mad, a mental case of extraordinary, mentally deranged powers, or He was what He said He was. No human being in his right mind can ever say, "I am the bread of life. He that eateth Me shall live forever." The person must be nuts. Suppose a human being stands up on Ben Yehuda Street (there *are* some cranks there, by the way) and says, "I am the bread of life. He that eateth Me shall live forever." You would say, "The man is crazy." But Jesus said it: "I am the bread of life. He that eateth Me shall abide in Me and I in Him. He that eateth My flesh shall live forever." It is no wonder that a number of disciples said, "No more; we are not having any more to do with this."

"I am the light of the world." Think of it. Can a human being say, "I am the light of the world; he that followeth Me shall not walk in darkness but shall have the light of life"? How can a human being say such a thing? "I am the light"—not I give light, or I point you to the light. "I am the light of the world. He that followeth Me shall not walk in darkness but shall have the light"—not of knowledge but the "light of life."

"I am the door." That sounds a bit weird doesn't it? Why doesn't He say, "I point you to the door"? "I am the good Shepherd." Okay, we can accept that. There is no claim to deity there.

"I am the resurrection and the life. He that believeth on Me, though he die yet shall he live, and he that liveth and believeth on Me shall never die." No man could say such a thing. I do not want to be blasphemous but Jesus must have been a nut case if He was not what He said He was. Now someone says, "You are making a lot out of that." No, I am not. The trouble with so many Christians is they have read these words since childhood, and they go in one ear and out the other. They run off them like water on a duck's back.

Think! "I am the bread of life; he that eateth Me shall live forever ... I am the resurrection and the life; he that believeth on Me, though he die, yet shall he live; and he that liveth and believeth on Me shall never die."

Here is the key: "Before Abraham was, I am." Do I have to tell you that the unmentionable name of God is "I AM that I

AM"? Moses said to the Lord when He appeared to him in that old dried-up thorn bush, "Whom shall I say sent me?" He said, "Say I AM has sent you."

I have heard many great preachers speak on the name of the Lord, I AM that I AM—His infinity, His omniscience, His omnipresence, His uncreatedness, His almighty power, Creator of heaven and earth. I have heard them all. But there was a little old Irishman who, when he was saved, could neither read nor write. He was a milkman in Dublin and learned to read and write because he wanted to read his Bible. His name was Johnny Cochran, and He became one of Ireland's greatest preachers. I heard him one day saying what I just said: "It leaves me cold, some of the sermons I have heard on this. After all I am just a little old man." He was a little old man with a stomach so large he used it as a lectern. He used to put his Bible on his stomach and flick over the pages as he preached.

He said, "I asked the Lord what this meant, and the Lord said to me, 'What I said to Moses, I say to you. I AM a blank check. You fill in what you need. Do you need grace? I AM grace. Do you need wisdom? I AM wisdom. Do you need power? I AM power.'" Johnny Cochran said it changed his life. It changed mine. Suddenly I understood. Jesus, the Word become flesh, takes this unmentionable name of the Lord and says, "I AM the bread of life. I AM the resurrection and the life. I AM the door. I AM the good shepherd. I AM the way, the truth, and the life. No man comes to the Father but by Me."

This is the most remarkable claim in my estimation: "I am the true vine and My Father is the husbandman." Any good Jew would know the vine is a symbol of Israel, a symbol of the people of God. Josephus tells us that there was a magnificent filigree gold vine right over the porch of the actual sanctuary, one of the great wonders of the ancient world. It signified the covenant people of God. How could Jesus say, "I am the people of God"? He must be mentally deranged or He is speaking the truth. No angel could say that. No created being could say that. Only God could say, "I am everything. I am the vine; you are in Me."

A vine is everything. I used to think that when the Lord said, "I am the vine, you are the branches" He meant, "I am the roots and you are the branches." But He never said that. He said, "I am the vine." And the vine is the roots, the trunk, the branches, the leaves, the tendrils, the blossom, and the fruit. The Lord was saying, "I am much greater than any of you, but you are in Me. And when you abide in Me and I in you, you bear much fruit." Who could have said such a thing unless it was the Word who became flesh?

This brings us to an inescapable conclusion. We are dealing with God. That Jesus was Man, I have no doubt. That Jesus grew weary, I have no doubt. That Jesus wept, I have no doubt. That Jesus thirsted, I have no doubt. That Jesus was overcome for a moment in the garden—not by the physical torture that lay ahead of Him, the physical death on the cross—but by the unknowable, when He who knew no sin would be made the sin of the world, I have no doubt. Jesus was human; I have no doubt about it. That is what I find so wonderful. I see that God has a color to His hair; He has a complexion to His face; He has color to His eyes; He is someone I understand. Jesus.

The Alpha and the Omega

In Hebrews 1:1–3a it says, "God, having of old time spoken unto the fathers in the prophets by divers portions and in divers manners, hath at the end of these days spoken unto us in his Son, whom he appointed heir of all things, through whom also he made the worlds; who being the effulgence of his glory [the radiant outshining of divine glory], and the very image of his substance, (the Greek word means the exact or precise impress of God's substance) and upholding all things by the word of his power."

Who is this? In Revelation 1:8 it says, "I am the Alpha and the Omega, saith the Lord God, who is and who was and who is to come, the Almighty." It is quite clear this is God Himself.

In Revelation 22:13 Jesus says, "I am the Alpha and the Omega, the first and the last, the beginning and the end." When the Lord Jesus said, "I am the Alpha and the Omega," they are the first and last letters of the Greek alphabet. In Hebrew it is, "I am the Aleph and the Tav." In English they say, "I am the A and the Zed," if you come from the proper English-speaking area. Otherwise you say, "A and Z." But when the Lord Jesus said, "I am the Alpha and Omega," did He mean He was only the first letter and the last letter of the alphabet? You cannot do anything with two letters of the alphabet. The whole point of an alphabet is to put thoughts or ideas into a defined, written, established form. And when the Lord Jesus said, "I am the Alpha and Omega," He was saying, "I am the alphabet of God. I am the language of God."

The Logos of God

Let me take you a step further. Here is the Word. It is the "logos" of God, the mind of God, the heart and the mind of God. Jesus is the way God speaks to us. Jesus is the way that God reveals Himself to us. Jesus is the way that God meets us in a way that we can understand. Jacob could never have wrestled with God because I think the very mystery of God's presence would have slain Him. But He wrestled with the One to whom Jacob said, "I will not let you go until you bless me." Afterwards he said, "I have seen the face of God and have lived." Many years later, Paul writing to the Corinthians spoke of "the knowledge of the glory of God in the face of Jesus the Messiah."

In Colossians it says, "We have been delivered out of the power of darkness, transferred into the kingdom of God's dear Son; in whom we have our redemption, the forgiveness of our sins: who is the image of the invisible God, the firstborn of all creation; for in Him were all things created, in the heavens and upon the earth, things visible, and things invisible, whether thrones or dominions or principalities or powers; all things have been created through Him, and unto Him; and he is before all things, and in him all things hold together."

There is an essential energy in the universe that so far scientists have been unable to define. They know it is there; they know it holds everything together, but none of us understands how. We can split the atom but the energy itself we as yet do not understand. That energy is the Lord Jesus. In Him the whole universe holds together. It will never break up until

God speaks the word. Then there will be a new heaven and a new earth wherein dwells righteousness. I find this tremendous.

Do you remember when Jesus died? Do you remember that terrible moment when he cried out, "My God, My God, why hast Thou forsaken Me?" A darkness came over the whole face of the earth. Unclever Christians say to us that it was an eclipse. No eclipse would ever last so many hours. It was something that happened to the basic energy of the universe. A sword went through the very heart of God, and in that moment the basic energy of the universe trembled and went dark. So great was the cost of your salvation and my salvation! No blood of goat or bull or heifer or lamb could ever do anything like that. In that moment when He, who fulfilled it all, became the sacrifice for our sin, something happened to the actual basic energy of the universe.

Are you going to tell me that Jesus is more than man and less than God? I am not asking you to start saying the creed or to try and define this thing for me. All I am saying is this: here you are face to face with something so infinite, so huge, so untellable, all I know is that God was in Christ, in the Messiah, reconciling the world.

"And he is the head of the body, the church, that in all things he might have the pre-eminence." Prominence is not pre-eminence. Did you hear that? Prominence is not pre-eminence. "That in *all* things He might have the pre-eminence." The fact that the Holy Spirit used the picture of head and body is in itself very interesting. You have never seen a living headless body, and you have never yet seen a living bodiless head. The Holy Spirit does not use this term "head and body" to picture the principal of a hospital, the principal of an academic institution, the chancellor of a university or something like that. So often it is understood in Christian circles that He is the head and we are sort of a corporation. No! Head and body are an organic whole, which means that God's idea of the church is union with Himself in the Messiah.

"That in all things he might have the pre-eminence." We need to dig this well and get the rubbish out of it so that the pure living water can flow again. If there is something in your life that He cannot have the pre-eminence in, get rid of it; it will destroy you. If there is something in our fellowship, in our church that cannot give the pre-eminence to the Lord Jesus, let's be done with it; it will destroy us.

The Epilogue

The second thing is as remarkable. This incredible gospel of John began with a prologue: "In the beginning was the Word, and the Word was with God, and the Word was God. And the Word became flesh and dwelt among us." And it ends with an epilogue.

Some people think it is just a little addendum. It is not. Jesus took one of the main characters in the story and said to him: "Peter, do you love Me more than these?"

The old Peter would have immediately said, "Of course! Lord, You know I love You more than all of them." He could not say it; he could not even rise to the same word. There are two words in Greek. He said, "Lord, You know I have an affection for You."

Then the Lord said to him, "Peter, do you love Me?" It was no longer "more than these." Peter had learned his lesson. "Now it is just you, Peter. Do you love Me?"

Peter said, "You know, Lord, I have an affection for You."

And the Lord said to him, "Peter, do you have an affection for Me?"

Peter said, "You know I do."

Why does this tremendous gospel, which interprets the Lord Jesus, end on this note? Beloved friends, beware of loveless Christianity. Beware of loveless service. Beware of loveless preaching. In the end it all comes down to this: if you have met God in the Lord Jesus, He is asking, "Do you love Me?"

You can work your fingers to the bone, but it does not satisfy the Lord. Love can never be satisfied by anything less, or other, than love. Your duty-bound work, your dutiful responsibility, your knowledge, your zeal, it means nothing in the end to the Lord. He chose Israel, He said, because He loved them. And when He said at the end of the old covenant, in the Christian arrangement, "Jacob I have loved," it is hard for many people to understand what it was that the Lord saw in Jacob. I think Jacob is sometimes, unfortunately, misrepresented as some kind of spineless, anemic, home-loving boy. I do not think he was that at all. I think he was a very tough man. Jacob had a heart for God. In spite of himself, in spite of his nature, and in spite of his sin, he had a heart for God.

You know the Lord stands among us even as we have talked about the Lord Jesus. God does not say to you, "Do you love the work?" He does not end this tremendous gospel by saying, "You know, I want you to get out and feed the sheep, tend the sheep, and look after the lambs." His first question is: "Do you love Me?" Then He says, "Get out and let this love for Me be the basis of your service."

I know some people get upset if I say anything about Catholics, but I must tell you this. I believe Mother Teresa gave to the world something that few other Christians have, and it was love.

I knew Malcolm Muggeridge as the most violent anti-monarchist, anti-church, anti-establishment atheist in a whole generation or more in Britain. With my own ears I heard him say, "I went to India to unmask Mother Teresa. I believed it was the normal, Christian missionary work. I did not think I was going to have any trouble unmasking her. But instead, when I went with her in the middle of the night to dying people on the streets of Calcutta and saw her kiss them, when the smell was so unbelievable and the maggots were eating their bodies, I knew for the first time I had seen a Christian."

Malcolm Muggeridge came back to Britain and went up to a monastery, of all things, in North Umbria. He did not go to services because he was still as anti-Catholic as ever. But after three weeks in a cell, Basil Hume, who became Cardinal Hume at Westminster, led him to the Lord. All the papers in Britain, those of you who are old enough to remember, said in their headlines: "Muggeridge Goes Senile!" I am not putting out a little bit of propaganda for the Catholic Church, I am talking about believers.

When you have a person, whoever it is, who is doing their service out of love for the Lord, it touches the unsaved. There is some kind of reality in it. Oh, that God would deliver us from this empty, cold, clinical Christianity and fill us with divine love. Then, once again the springs of living water will flow out. From within shall flow out rivers of living water, changing everything, bringing life to everything, and creating fruit.

May God help us. We have looked at the Person of the Lord Jesus. I would never be able to put into words how I understand the triune nature of God. I know I have a little finite mind and my intelligence has very definite boundaries. But I also know that in my spirit I have met the Father in the Lord Jesus. I always address all my prayers to the Father in the name of the Lord Jesus. Somehow I understand what little I can in my finite being. I understand God in the Lord Jesus. He relates to me and I to Him.

May God touch our hearts. May the Lord visit you and visit me, touch our hearts in the quietness of the night hours, and come to us with those words: "Do you love Me?"

2.
The Word of God

John 17:17

Sanctify them in the truth: thy word is truth.

Isaiah 40:6–8

The voice of one saying, Cry. And one said, What shall I cry? All flesh is grass, and all the goodliness thereof is as the flower of the field. The grass withereth, the flower fadeth, because the breath of the Lord bloweth upon it; surely the people is grass. The grass

withereth, the flower fadeth; but the word of our God shall stand forever.

Hebrews 4:12–13

For the word of God is living, and active, and sharper than any two-edged sword, and piercing even to the dividing of soul and spirit, of both joints and marrow, and quick to discern the thoughts and intents of the heart. And there is no creature that is not manifest in his sight: but all things are naked and laid open before the eyes of him with whom we have to do.

II Timothy 3:14–16

But abide thou in the things which thou hast learned and hast been assured of knowing of whom thou hast learned them; and that from a child thou hast known the sacred writings which are able to make thee wise unto salvation through faith which is in Christ Jesus. Every scripture inspired of God is also profitable for teaching, for reproof, for correction, for instruction which is in righteousness: that the man of God may be complete, furnished completely unto every good work.

I Peter 1:22–25

Seeing you have purified your souls in your obedience to the truth unto unfeigned love of the brethren, love one another from the heart fervently: having been begotten again, not of corruptible seed, but of incorruptible, through the word of God, which liveth and abideth. For, all flesh is as grass, and all the glory thereof as the flower of grass. The grass withereth, and the flower falleth: but the word of the Lord abideth forever.

Shall we pray:

Beloved Lord, we are so thankful that You are here and that in this time we can very simply turn to You. We thank You for the anointing, which You have provided for the ministry of Your word, not only for the speaking of Your word, but for the hearing of Your word and the translating of Your word. Into that anointing we stand by faith. Fill this time with Yourself, with Your speaking and working. And we shall be careful to give You all the praise and all the glory. We ask it in the name of our Messiah, the Lord Jesus. Amen.

The theme of these days has been "The Battle for the Truth." The burden that is on my heart is the word of God because the battle for the truth is essentially a battle for the word of God in all its fulness and power.

Whenever the word of God has been unshackled and has become free, whenever it has been put into the language, the mother tongue of the people, whenever it has been freely preached, tremendous things have happened. The direction and character of whole nations have been changed. It does not matter whether you go to the Old Testament when Hezekiah found the book of the law, or when Josiah found the book of the law, or Ezra and Nehemiah read the book of the law, every time the word of God has been rediscovered, there has been a rediscovering of the power of God. It is the power of God to save, the power of God to change the course of history, the power of God to produce real, eternal, spiritual character. You can never underestimate the value of the word of God. Therefore, I believe that what we are dealing with is of supreme importance.

The Battle for Intercession

We can talk about the truth of intercession. Where do we find real intercession today? It is a lost art in the church of God. Most of our prayer meetings are babblings. Most of our prayer meetings are a whole collection of petitions and requests. There is nothing wrong with petitions and requests, but where is the intercession? There is a battle for intercession, and so far the battle has been lost. Entertainment has taken the place. Affluence has done its deadly work amongst the people of God. Where you find real intercession is in the suffering church in mainland China and in the suffering church still in Muslim countries, where there are faithful men and women who know how to pray together and pray things through together. But in countries like Britain and the United States, with all the marvelously well-oiled spiritual machinery we call the church, where is intercession? It is lost.

There was a reason why the apostle Paul ended the Ephesian letter, containing perhaps the high-water mark of revelation, not with an appeal for Bible teaching, or for more evangelism, or for the deepening of spiritual life, all of which are essential and important. He ended it with a cry that men and women might learn how to put on the whole armor of God and stand and withstand and having done all, to stand.

The Battle for the Person of the Lord Jesus

There is the battle for the person of the Lord Jesus—His centrality, His supremacy, His pre-eminence. What a battle there is over the person of the Lord Jesus! If that battle is lost, everything is lost.

You will never, ever know who the Lord Jesus is apart from the word of God. It is through the word of God, and the Spirit of God working upon the word of God, that we see light in His light. We come face to face with the mystery of the person of the Lord

Jesus in whom the Father has placed everything—salvation, eternal life, spiritual growth, glory, and power. It is all in Him.

The Battle for the Church

I think of the battle for the church. What a mess we have made of the church! Beloved brothers and sisters, what a mess we have made of the church. I was a rabid Baptist. When I was in Egypt I tried to make every single one I led to the Lord a good Baptist. I have nothing against the Baptists. I think it is absolutely tremendous. what God has done through the Anabaptists. There are places like beautiful Salzburg where Anabaptists were drowned in every single fountain in that city. Men, women, and children were sewn up in sacks and drowned. It is no wonder I was a rabid Baptist. I knew their history when I first came to the Lord. But on the day that I saw what the church was as the body of Christ, my Baptist fervor died and I became a believer, just a brother amongst brethren. I never thought anything would cause such a fuss as my ceasing to be a Baptist. I am not saying that if you are a Baptist, you should cease to be a Baptist. But for me, I cannot be a Lutheran. I cannot be a Wesleyan. We say we are Calvinists, but that is in theology. Otherwise, I am not a Calvinist either. I am a "bit"; I am a bit of everything. I thank God for baptism by immersion as a believer. I thank God for the new birth and entire sanctification of the Methodists. I thank God for elders of the Presbyterians. I thank God for so many things.

We are in an enormous battle for the church. Why? It is because the word of God says, "The bride will make herself ready." Satan picks up things. Thank God he does not know everything, but he comes to prayer meetings; he comes to a meeting like this and listens. He works through his whole intelligence service. He has to stop that bride from making herself ready or it is his end. And he will do everything in his power to stop it. What a battle for the truth of the church! If we are going to see something in the last days, even if it is only in a remnant of believers who are faithful to the Lord, sometimes the Lord has to allow persecution to sweep away the whole Christian organization, the whole top-heavy thing. Then the organic may develop and the real life of the Messiah shared by those who are saved, together, may become manifest. It would be so much easier if we could do it without the persecution. But the Lord has an agenda and if He can do it no other way, He will do it that way.

The Battle for Israel

And what a battle there is for Israel! I believe with all my heart that the truth concerning Israel is essential to the health of the church. That is why there is such a battle for this matter. By and large people pour scorn upon this matter, including preachers, ministers, pastors, and teachers as if it belongs to a bunch of nutcases, spiritual fanatics, people who are overboard. Well, I have to say after long experience that we do have nutcases, fanatics, and people who are overboard. But I want to know what people mean when they say we are radical. I say we are normal. It is the truth of God's word.

If I had the time, I would go back to Scriptures that I believe are unassailable, incontrovertible—Scriptures like Jeremiah 31. How do you apply that to the church? What does it say about

Samaria? What does it say about planting vineyards on the mountains of Samaria? No one ever planted vineyards on the mountains of Samaria when they came back from Nebuchadnezzar's exile. You know that from Jesus. You know that the woman of Samaria said to Him, "What is it that you, a Jew, speaks to a woman who is a Samaritan?" The Jews and Samaritans had no dealings with each other. Don't they know their Bibles? It is the battle for the truth.

People tell me that it was all finished when they came back from the exile in Babylon under Nebuchadnezzar. I say that is nonsense, absolute nonsense! Furthermore, not buried in the New Testament, but in the greatest exposition of the gospel in the whole sixty-six books of the Bible, the Roman letter, in chapter 11 you have those marvelous words: "And so all Israel shall be saved." He speaks about the great divine agenda to bring the gospel to the ends of the earth to every tongue, to every tribe, to every nation, to every ethnic group. Out of them He will take a people for Himself and then He will turn again to the Jewish people. Multitudes and multitudes of Jews will come to saving faith in God through the finished work of the Messiah, Jesus. That is a battle for the truth.

The Authority of the Word

This whole matter of the word of God is essential, and it is an enormous battle. So I have some questions. Is the word of God authoritative? And if it is authoritative, how much of it is authoritative? Is it *all* authoritative?

Is the word of God relevant? Is it relevant to modern society, to the norms of modern society?

Is it *all* inspired of God? Or are there certain passages that have managed to get within these sixty-six books that are uninspired, or less inspired?

Does it still have power? The Lord Jesus, in what we call His high priestly prayer, as recorded in John 17, said, "Sanctify them in the truth. Thy word is truth." It is not just a recognition of the theology of God's word, although good theology and sound doctrine are important. It is not just a question of recognizing the word of God as the word of God. Something happens. "Sanctify them in the truth." It is not enough to recognize the word of God. It is whether you are prepared for the Holy Spirit to take the word of God and do something in your life, in your circumstances, in your family, in your business, in your communities, in your nation.

"Sanctify them in the truth. Thy word is truth." What is the word of God? Is it all sixty-six books that make up the Bible or is it only twenty-seven? I have never been able to understand people who think that the twenty-seven writings of the New Testament are so relevant, so authoritative, so inspired, all of which were completed two thousand years ago, but apparently feel that which was another two or three thousand years earlier is somehow or other suspect.

People tell me that we Jews exaggerate, that in order to state a case, we overstate it. I find it very strange that the New Testament was written by Jewish hands, but they do not seem to think that. People seem to think that a new breed, a new ethnic group developed, that we are somehow or other free from this dreadful Jewish tendency.

Has the word of God been compromised? What do I mean? Did some dozy scribe, in the stupor of a Middle East heat, manage to get things into the Scripture that should not be there? In other words, you cannot completely trust the word of God as it is because we do not know whether people put little bits and pieces in, or added pieces or took things out. I call them dozy scribes.

Let me put it another way. Is the word of God culturally in a straightjacket? In other words, there are a whole lot of things in the word of God, including the New Testament, that are apparently cultural. We do not have to bother about them. Baptizing people by immersion is a dreadfully vulgar way of baptizing. It is much nicer to sprinkle a little bit of water on somebody's head, or even to make the sign of the cross. How very sophisticated! It is sort of pleasant. I do not want to upset people. I know some of you may have been baptized that way, and I do not want to cause problems with anybody. Archaeologically, we have discovered from the baptisteries that people either went right down into the water or they poured buckets of water over them. We know that even from the Didache, the teaching of the twelve: "Let them be baptized fully in water, and if there is not enough, let them take a jug and pour it over them. And if there is not enough for a jug of water, sprinkle them."

As time went on, the gospel went farther north to the Scandinavian and German countries, where they live in ice and snow for half the year with polar bears running around. Of course, it was much better to sprinkle. You did not want someone who was being baptized to catch their death of cold.

I use that only as an illustration. For instance, I am told that the apostle said something about women wearing something on their heads when they pray. "Oh," people say, "that is totally cultural. We do not have to worry about that." Okay, do not worry about it, but let me just say this. There is one little phrase there that you ought to take note of: "because of the angels." I have heard again and again that it is cultural. So what else is cultural? Shall we throw this out? Who will decide what is cultural and what is not cultural?

The Beginning and End of the Bible

In the Bible, there is a beginning and an end. I remember the day I discovered this. It was through Dr. Graham Scroggie that I first began to get a glimpse of it, and then through that amazing brother from India, Bakht Singh. And I wondered, "Can this be true?" I went back to the Bible and I began to look at it, and the more I looked at it the more excited I became. How could it possibly be that the first three chapters of Genesis and the last three chapters of John in Revelation exactly correspond? There was a tree of life and a tree of life; a river of life and a river of life; two people in the garden and at the end a multitude that nobody could number; in the beginning the Lord visiting once a day in the cool of the day, and in the end the Lord dwelling there forever. The correspondence is minute.

In the first two chapters and the last two chapters of the Bible, you have the beginning and the end of the matter without sin and without the fall. In Genesis 3 and Revelation 20, you have sin coming in and Satan cast out into the bottomless pit forever and ever. It is the beginning and the end. That is amazing, especially since the book of Revelation was questioned for four hundred years as to whether it should be in the canon of Scripture. There were all kinds of doubts about it. Should it be in the canon of Scripture? Should it not be in the canon of Scripture? It seemed to be a little too fanciful. In the end, it came to the last place in the canon of Scripture and occupied the place it should occupy by divine right.

If the beginning of the Bible and the end of the Bible so minutely correspond, what does that say for the canon of Scripture? It means, in my estimation, that the sixty-six books of the Bible are a complete revelation of God. Whether you understand it or not is another matter. It is the complete, final revelation of the mind and the heart of God.

The Centre of the Bible

If you open the Bible to the center, to the heart of the Bible, you come to two extraordinary little books—Ecclesiastes, which in Hebrew is "the Preacher," and the Song of Songs. For years they argued about these two little books, especially Ecclesiastes, because it just does not seem to be in line with the rest of God's word. It seems, for those of you who know anything about philosophy, to be existentialism. Jean Paul Sartre—"Eat, drink, and be merry, for tomorrow we die." "Vanity, vanity, all is vanity." Or to put it another way: "Emptiness, emptiness, all is emptiness." "Stupidity, stupidity, all is stupidity."

There in the middle of it is one little word: "And God has set eternity in their heart, yet so that man cannot find out the work that God hath done from the beginning even to the end" (Ecclesiastes 3:11b). In other words, in every human being there is an eternal vacuum—a vacuum that you can fill with the things of time and sense, but which will never satisfy you.

Then there is the Song of Songs, and liberal theologians call it a bawdy ditty that should not be in the word of God; a disgusting picture. In our Jewish tradition it is an allegory, given in vision to Solomon of the love of God for Israel. Now, it is "Purpose, purpose, all is purpose." Now, it is "Value, value, all is value." This is the heart of your Bible.

The Living Word

Are you going to tell me that there are parts of this book that we should dispense with? Some people tell me that the whole Old Testament is obsolete and you should not read it. We will read little bits of Isaiah and Psalms, but the rest of it is obsolete; it belongs to history. It is gone, finished. It is strange that the Lord should have given us thirty-nine books that are obsolete. No! In my estimation, the word of God is the word of God. It is the canon of Scripture, a word from the Hebrew meaning "to rule, something cut off, something measured." God gave us the canon of Scripture so that we are not left to our own subjective ideas, emotions, and reasonings. Whether we understand it or not, it is the mind and the heart of God revealed. And Jesus, blessed be His name, is the personification of that word. No wonder He is called the Word, the Word who became flesh and dwelt among us, in whom we beheld the glory of God. Is it any wonder?

The church is not something apart from the Lord Jesus; it is in Him. It is His body—Head and body. If you separate a head and body, you have a dead head and a dead body. That is the whole point of this amazing figure that Jesus is Head and we are the body. We are in a living whole. We function in life together. It is amazing. It is in Him. The Lord Jesus is the whole sixty-six books of the Bible expressed—the very heart of God revealed. He is the very mind of God revealed in terms that you and I can understand. There is a color to the hair, a color to the eyes, a complexion to the skin, a body that we can relate to.

And let me tell you a secret about Israel. Israel may at present be divorced from the Lord. She may be alienated from the Lord, but the whole meaning of Israel is that in the sight of God she is in the Messiah. In the end she will return where she belongs. And if the Lord has to use the nations to drive her there, He will use the nations to drive her there. If He has to knock out every single prop that she leans upon, He will knock it away. If He has to devastate her so that in her weakness and in her sorrow she has no one to turn to, then she will find the Messiah and into the arms of God she will fall.

The Apostles' Doctrine

In Acts 2:42 it says, "And they continued steadfastly in the apostles' doctrine." What is the apostles' doctrine? In every theological seminary I visit, I normally cause a lot of trouble and leave a trail of damage. But the reason I do is because I love to be able to say to them that the early church had no New Testament. People seem to think that it had the New Testament and studied the letters of the apostle Paul or James. They never had it. Where did they get all these great evangelical doctrines? They got them from the thirty-nine books of the Old Testament. Jesus, the Master, the Head of the church, opened the understanding of those two on the road to Emmaus from Moses and the first five books, the prophets, and the writings—all things concerning Himself. He was the center of it. That is what I meant when I said that Jesus is the personification of the Word of God. It was not hard for the Lord Jesus to say, "Here I am. Do you see the tree that they threw into the pool of Marah? That was Me. Do you understand the pillar of cloud and the pillar of fire? That was Me. Do you understand the manna? That was Me. Don't you understand?"

I do not believe a single one of those apostles had the slightest doubt about the authority, the inspiration, and the relevance of the thirty-nine books of the Old Testament. I even say in Baptist Bible schools and seminaries that since there was no Roman letter and no Romans 6, they even found baptism in Isaiah's prophecy. When the Ethiopian eunuch got baptized, where did Philip find it? He was reading in Isaiah, and somehow from Isaiah, he led the eunuch to see that he needed to be saved. When he asked the Lord to be his Lord and his Savior, he said straightaway, "Where is there water that I may be baptized?" What a tremendous thing happened in Ethiopia as a result of the Ethiopian eunuch!

If you look at the New Testament, everything was written by the apostles, their close associates, Luke and Mark, or the Lord's two brothers, James and Jude. What else have you got left? We have the Hebrew letter. Who wrote the Hebrew letter? I have always believed that it was Apollos, but that is my own view.

God's word is complete. It is divine, it is relevant, and it is practical. That means God can take a phrase from Genesis and do something in your life by the Holy Spirit. Have you ever had that experience while reading the Word? Suddenly, it jumps out as if it is alive. It *is* alive. That is the whole point. It is alive. It grips you. You can never be the same again. If you have never had such an experience, I feel sorry for you. Are you born again?

I remember when I asked Mr. Sparks about the Charismatics. I thought he would say, "Humph," but no, he said, "It is of God." Then he said, "But I want to tell you that what they call the baptism of the Spirit, I think it is that they are all getting born again. Half of them were saved in the head, objectively. Now they are born again. And the evidence is that they hunger for the Lord; they thirst for the Lord; they long for fellowship."

All Scripture is Inspired by God

Paul said to Timothy in II Timothy, "You know that through the sacred writings, you have been made wise to salvation." What a beautiful way of putting it. "All Scripture," he said, "is inspired of God and is profitable," meaning of course, at that time, the thirty-nine books of the Old Covenant. Then he goes on to tell us how it is profitable. He says, "It is profitable for teaching, for reproof, for correction, for instruction which is in righteousness, that the man of God may be complete." Some of the modern versions say, and I think well, "qualified." Then it goes on to say, "completely equipped unto every good work."

How can you be completely equipped unto every good work? You say straightaway, "By the Holy Spirit," and I agree. But it is through the Holy Spirit's illumination of the word of God. Be careful of anything that is extra-biblical. But the Holy Spirit can take this book—whether it is a Psalm, or Isaiah, or Jeremiah, or Obadiah, or Haggai, or Leviticus—and illuminate it. Some people avoid Leviticus like the plague. Oh, what a wonderful book it is! The Lord Jesus is the five-fold offering. Wonderful! The fact of the matter is that we have something tremendous here.

What is all this nonsense I hear that Paul is the founder of Christianity? Where does this come from, that Paul is the founder of Christianity? It is tripe, absolute tripe. I am ashamed of anyone who says such a thing, as if somehow or other Paul is slightly off-color. He should never have done it.

What is all this talk about Paul being a woman-hater? I hear it again and again in Evangelical circles. "He is a woman-hater," I am told. "Look at him; he had no feeling for women." Poor Paul. It is true that he said, "It is better for a man never to have touched a woman," but that does not mean that he was a woman-hater. I think the apostle Paul was one of the greatest champions of women in the Bible. And I think what he said about the need for women to be very, very careful should be listened to by every sister because women have tremendous power, far greater than men. We like to think that men have the power, but men do not have the power. Women have the power.

Satan has supreme intelligence, outside of God. He is so intelligent. Why do you think he went for Eve? Why didn't he go for Adam? Adam was too dull, too stupid. He would probably have looked at the fruit and said, "I'd rather have a hamburger."

Satan went for Eve because he knew that if he got Eve he had Adam, and that is exactly what he is doing now. He is going

for the women of the world, especially in western countries—
the whole feminist movement. Of course, I realize that women
have had a very hard deal. Why should a woman be paid a third
less for doing as much work as a man? Why should women not
be allowed to vote? It is unbelievable, isn't it? But having said all
that, the fact of the matter is, that Satan is going for the women.
If he is going to win (and he believes he still has a chance to win),
he is going to go for the women.

How wonderful this is: "The word of our God shall stand
forever." The Hebrew there is very interesting. Our versions say,
"shall stand." Some of the modern versions say, "shall endure."
But it is a word that actually means "to arise" as well as "to stand."
It has the feeling that this word of God is not something merely
impassive, something, if I may put it this way, dead, static.
It is alive. It is alive!

The Word is Living

"The word of God is living and active and sharper than any two-
edged sword." Isn't that a wonderful word? Living. The word
of God is living. In other words, when God says, "Let there be
light," there is light. When God spoke, things were created out
of nothing. They had no pre-existence. God can do anything.
His word is so tremendous. It is living, creative.

Shakespeare, even *The Taming of the Shrew*, has never healed a
marriage. Have the words of Goethe or Schiller ever leapt into a
human life and saved them from alcoholism, from drug addiction,
from suicide, from misery? No! But when the Holy Spirit takes

the word of God and gets it into a human life, suddenly a person smiles and is full of light.

I remember years ago, a fellow from Chile who was a rugby player. He had a chin like an anvil. When the door opened, his chin came in first. And this dear sister who was my doctor, said to me, "I want you to talk with him. He needs to find the Lord."

And I said, "My dear sister, I would do anything for you. You know that very well. You have kept me so well and alive through the years, but I will never try to get somebody saved. That is God's job. If the opportunity comes, I will speak with him."

So I refused to speak to him. I could not believe it, but this great, big ox-like fellow sat through meeting after meeting. And I thought, "What does he get out of it? What has my dear doctor done dragging this poor fellow into these meetings? It is enough to kill anybody." (For us who were the Lord's, we were getting something.)

Then I will never forget when he walked through the door one day. Instantly, I knew he was saved. Light shone through that anvil chin of his. It actually made him handsome, beautiful. Somehow, an inner light had been switched on. He had been born again through the living and enduring word of God. What a tremendous thing it is when the word of God gets inside of a human being and they are saved and made one with God in the Messiah! Isn't it tremendous?

And it doesn't stop there. Every single step forward is a further discovery of the Lord through His word. I feel so sorry for the situation we have in the church now. It is no wonder it is on the brink of apostasy. I go places where young people have never even read the letter of James, ever. I go to places where they have never even heard of Obadiah or Haggai. What is wrong?

We have swung from Word-oriented Christianity to experience-oriented Christianity. There is nothing wrong with that. Before, we had dead Bible studies. Dead, dead, dead! They were so dead you had to haul yourself in to them and at the end you crawled out of them. But now it is all experience, experience, experience. And some of the experiences, I think, are questionable. But the Holy Spirit always takes the word of God and illuminates it.

That is why the apostle Paul, writing to the church at Ephesus, said, "My prayer for you is that God may give to you the spirit of wisdom and revelation in the knowledge of Him, the eyes of your heart being enlightened that you may know what is the hope of His calling." It is living, active, sharper than any two-edged sword, dividing between soul and spirit. Isn't that a tremendous thing?

So much of our Christianity today is humanistic. Our souls—our reasonings, our emotions, and our wills—are in charge of the word of God. It is only what we will that we will accept from the word of God, only what titillates us, only what satisfies our reasoning powers.

The Word Divides Soul and Spirit

What a tremendous thing it is when the Holy Spirit divides between soul and spirit and uncovers the thoughts and intents of our hearts—the motivating factors, the real, essential, motivating factors.

Do you remember the ten spies? They went, they saw, and their reasoning powers got on top. Then their emotions came into it, and then their will. They came back and said, "It is a wonderful land, but the men are giants." (They did not say anything about the women, but I take it there were giant women as well.) And they said, "The cities are walled up to heaven; we cannot take it."

Two spies said, "Yes, they are walled up to heaven and there are giants, but we can take it." What was the difference? It was the word of God that made the difference. The two spies believed that what God had said about the Angel of His Presence going before and driving them out was real. The Lord meant exactly what He said. All they had to do was use the soles of their feet and the Lord would do the rest. That is exactly the context in Hebrews 4, because it says through unbelief they all died in the wilderness.

When God's word is given the place it ought to have in a personal life, individual life, family life, business life, church life, in the work of the Lord, and the lives of the workers, something always happens. It is as simple as that.

Obedience to the Truth

I want to end with that word of Peter, the apostle: "Seeing you have purified your souls to obedience of the truth."

If I were asked what is the greatest problem we have amongst Christian believers, I would say straightaway it is this: Are you the master of God's word? Are you the controller of His word? Or are you obedient?

It is interesting how the apostle Peter puts it here in this Scripture. "Seeing you have purified your souls in your obedience to the truth." And the word in Greek is the idea of a cleansing for a living sacrifice. In other words, your soul is in its right place. When a believer is in the right place, then the Lord is in their spirit controlling soul and body.

Have you ever noticed how the Psalmist says, "Be still my soul"? I used to think: Is he a schizophrenic? What is wrong with him? Who is speaking to whom? "Be still my soul." "I have quieted my soul like a weaned child." Who is speaking to whom? Is his soul speaking to his soul? It is like a kind of spiritual schizophrenic. Here he is, saying to himself, "Sh-h-h-h-h."

No, the Psalmist understood more than many believers in the new covenant. His spirit was saying to his soul, "Shut up. Be still. Be quiet. Don't wail all the time, whine all the time, murmur all the time. Be still."

It is a wonderful thing to get to know the word of God. I thank God that when I was first saved, I was saved amongst a people who believed in the authority of God's word and the power of God's word. And they lived it, maybe rather poorly, but they lived it.

When I went to Egypt, I saw those two extraordinary old sisters, for whom I thank the Lord on bended knee. They taught me about intercession, and I have never forgotten them. They were like walking Bibles. They knew the most obscure portions. I was usually very outspoken, always ready to say what I thought and tell them where I thought they were wrong and all the rest of it. But after a while I kept my mouth shut because I could not believe it. I would mention Obadiah, and those ladies knew that book of Obadiah, inside out, and Haggai, and everything else. And when they went to prayer, that is what they stood on—all kinds of Scriptures. It revolutionized my whole attitude. I never knew that anyone could know the Bible like that and live it.

Dear brother, dear sister, here is a battle, a battle for the truth. We have an institutional church now that is so going off in the wrong way, with gay bishops living in sin with gay partners, being consecrated as such—God help us. We should expect it. I know that sounds very mean of me to say, but we should expect it.

I remember the Bishop of Durham, years ago saying, "The resurrection is nothing but a cheap conjuring trick with bones." I remember the Bishop of Birmingham saying on another occasion that Jesus undoubtedly had a sexual relationship with Mary Magdalene. This was years ago, so we should expect all this kind of thing. But what saddens me is the real church of God, those who ought to know the word of God, but do not; those who should be having a living experience of the Lord through the word of God by the Holy Spirit, but are not. That saddens me. I see young people who are not memorizing the word of God. Memorizing the word of God in itself will not do anything, but it is material that is the foundation for the Holy Spirit to bring things back into your memory again and again and again.

We need to be men and women subject to the authority of God's word. We need to be men and women who recognize the relevance of God's word in all its parts. We need to be people who understand that the word of God is intensely practical. It comes right down to the most ordinary, mundane matters.

We need to be people of whom it can be said, the word of the Messiah dwells in them—not visiting them, not using them, but dwelling in them. May it be so; that is my prayer.

Shall we pray:

Deliver this time in any sense from being misunderstood, but help us to understand exactly what was said, even if it has somewhat shocked us. We need to be people of Your word. We need to be people in whom the word has become, as it were, flesh and blood. It is dwelling in us in all wisdom—what a wonderful word, in all wisdom. We need to be people who have received the implanted word—it is taking root, growing up, and bearing fruit. We need to be people, Lord, where the truth has set us free—free from ourselves, free from bondages, free to serve You. Lord, hear us. What a battle there is over the word of God! And how this mystery of lawlessness, which at its heart contradicts Your word, grows and makes inroads into those who are children of God! Deliver us, O Lord. Deliver us. Let that word of the Lord Jesus be fulfilled in us, "Sanctify them, set them apart, separate them from the world through the truth. Your word is truth." Do it, Lord. We ask it in the name of our Lord, Jesus. Amen.

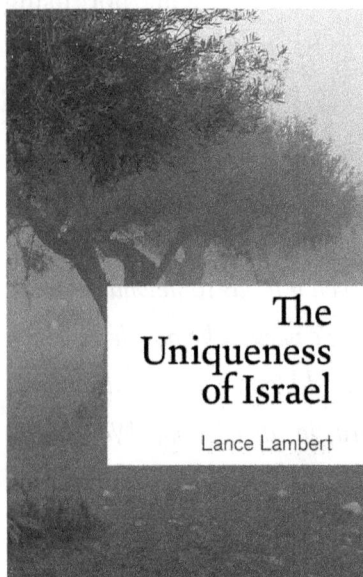

The Uniqueness of Israel

Woven into the fabric of Jewish existence there is an undeniable uniqueness. There is bitter controversy over the subject of Israel, but time itself will establish the truth about this nation's place in God's plan. For Lance Lambert, the Lord Jesus is the key that unlocks Jewish history He is the key not only to their fall, but also to their restoration. For in spite of the fact that they rejected Him, He has not rejected them.

Till the Day Dawns

"And we have the word of prophecy made more sure; whereunto ye do well that ye take heed, as unto a lamp shining in a dark place, until the day dawn, and the day-star arise in your hearts." (II Peter 1:9).

The word of prophecy was not given that we might merely be comforted but that we would be prepared and made ready. Let us look into the Word of God together, searching out the prophecies, that the Day-Star arise in our hearts until the Day dawns.

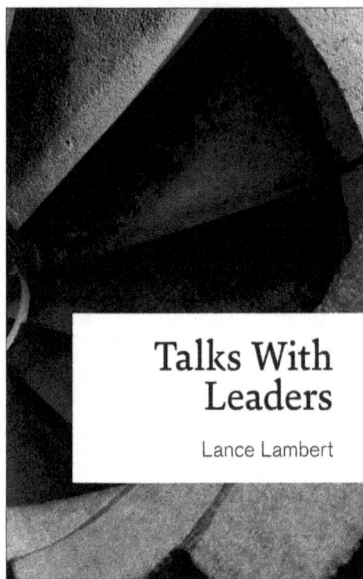

Talks With Leaders

Lance Lambert

Talks With Leaders

"O Timothy, guard that which is committed unto thee ..." (1 Timothy 6:20) Has God given you something? Has God deposited something in you? Is there something of Himself which He has given to you to contribute to the people of God? Guard it. Guard that vision which He has given you. Guard that understanding that He has so mercifully granted to you. Guard that experience which He has given that it does not evaporate or drain away or become a cause of pride. Guard that which the Lord has given to you by the Holy Spirit. In these heart-to-heart talks with leaders Lance Lambert covers such topics as the character of God's servants, the way to serve, the importance of anointing, and hearing God's voice. Let us consider together how to remain faithful with what has been entrusted to us.

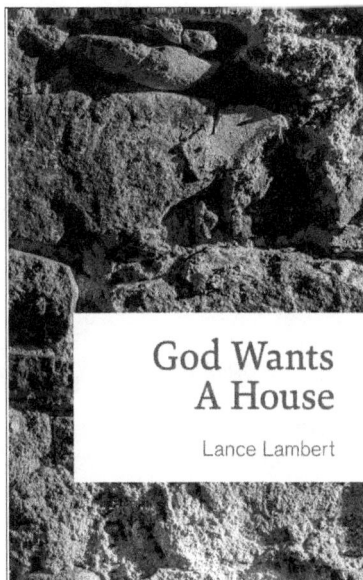

God Wants a House

Where is God at home? Is He at home in Richmond, VA?
Is He at home in Washington? Is He at home in Richmond, Surrey?
Is He at home in these other places? Where is God at home? There
are thousands of living stones, many, many dear believers with
real experience of the Lord, but where has the ark come home?
Where are the staves being lengthened that God has finally come
home? In God Wants a House Lance looks into this desire of the
Lord, this desire He has to dwell with His people. What would
this dwelling look like? Let's seek the Lord, that we can say with
David, "One thing have I asked of Jehovah, that will I seek after:
that I may dwell in the house of Jehovah all the days of my life,
To behold the beauty of Jehovah, And to inquire in his temple."